GREAT ZOOS OF THE UNITED STATES™

SAN DIEGO ZOO

CLAUDIA PEARCE AND KAREN E. WORLEY
Zoological Society of San Diego

The Rosen Publishing Group's
PowerKids Press™
New York

Published in 2003 by The Rosen Publishing Group, Inc.
29 East 21st Street, New York, NY 10010

First Edition

Editor: Natashya Wilson
Book Design: Michael J. Caroleo and Michael de Guzman

Photo Credits: All photographs by Zoological Society of San Diego.

Pearce, Claudia.
  San Diego Zoo / Claudia Pearce and Karen E. Worley ; photography by Ken Bohn and Ron Garrison.— 1st ed.
        v. cm. — (Great zoos of the United States)
    Includes bibliographical references (p.   ).
    Contents: It began with a roar — The world-famous zoo — Making animals feel at home — The San Diego Zoo's most famous baby — In the reptile house — Karen's heart — Playing, thinking, and learning — This is wild — Wild and weird animal facts — Saving animals.
    ISBN 0-8239-6321-7 (lib. bdg.)
    1. San Diego Zoo—Juvenile literature. [1. San Diego Zoo. 2. Zoos.] I. Worley, Karen E. II. Bohn, Ken, ill. III. Garrison, Ron, ill. IV. Title. V. Series.
  QL76.5.U62 S267 2003
  590'.7'3794985—dc21
                                                    2002000522

Manufactured in the United States of America

Contents

1 It Began with a Roar 5

2 The World-Famous Zoo 6

3 Making Animals Feel at Home 9

4 The San Diego Zoo's Most Famous Baby 10

5 In the Reptile House 13

6 Karen's Heart 14

7 Playing, Thinking, and Learning 17

8 This Is Wild! 18

9 Wild and Weird Animal Facts 21

10 Saving Animals 22

Glossary 23

Index 24

Web Sites 24

When the Zoo started, there were hardly any trees or plants. Dr. Wegeforth rode around on his horse and poked seeds into the ground with his cane to plant them!

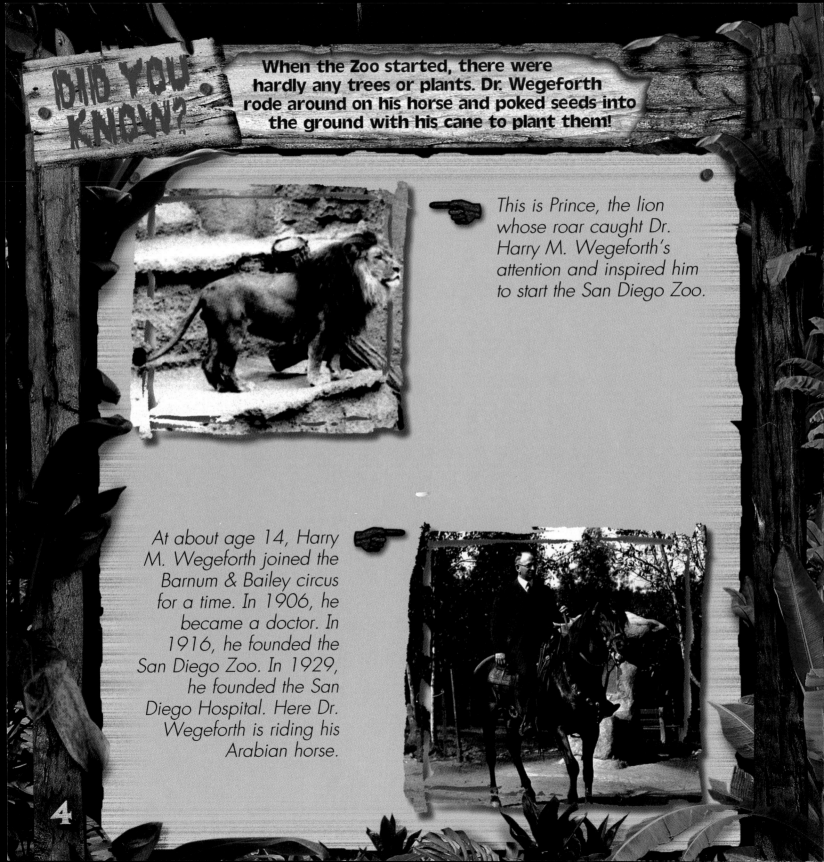

This is Prince, the lion whose roar caught Dr. Harry M. Wegeforth's attention and inspired him to start the San Diego Zoo.

At about age 14, Harry M. Wegeforth joined the Barnum & Bailey circus for a time. In 1906, he became a doctor. In 1916, he founded the San Diego Zoo. In 1929, he founded the San Diego Hospital. Here Dr. Wegeforth is riding his Arabian horse.

Without a lion named Prince, San Diego, California, might not have a world-famous zoo. In 1915, a huge fair called the Panama-California International Exposition was held in San Diego. One of the **exhibits** included lions, monkeys, and bears. After the fair was over, the animals stayed, living in their cages in a field that is now Balboa Park.

One day a doctor named Harry M. Wegeforth drove by with his brother. They were startled by a loud, spine-tingling roar. It was Prince the lion. That gave Dr. Wegeforth an idea. "Wouldn't it be splendid if San Diego had a zoo!" he said to his brother. "You know, I think I'll start one." That's just what he did, all because Prince roared!

THE WORLD-FAMOUS ZOO

It started small, but the San Diego Zoo is a big deal today. It is 100 acres (40 ha) in size, about the size of 60 football fields! More than 3 million people visit it every year. They come to see the more than 800 **species** and **subspecies** of animals in the Zoo. Some of these species are **endangered**.

It takes many people to run the Zoo. More than 1,000 people work there. Even more people work there in the summer, when the crowds are bigger. Everyone works for the sake of the animals, but not everyone is an animal keeper. The Zoo also has architects, accountants, chefs, gardeners, teachers, scientists, writers, and other workers. Imagine all there would be to do if you ran the Zoo!

The San Diego Zoo is also a garden with many rare and endangered plant species. In fact, some of the plants are more endangered than the animals!

A bush shaped like an elephant grows by the entrance to the Zoo.

Bottom: *Sometimes the otters climb small trees to play with their swamp monkey friends.*

Sometimes the guenons reach down from a tree to try to pat a forest buffalo!

8

MAKING ANIMALS FEEL AT HOME

The San Diego Zoo often has different animal species living together, just as they would in the wild. This makes the animals feel more at home. For example, monkeys, otters, and forest buffalo all live together in the Ituri **tropical rain forest** in Africa, so they also live together in the Zoo's Ituri Forest exhibit in the southwest area of the Zoo. They enjoy playing with one another. The swamp monkeys play in the water with the otters and sometimes even take rides on the otters' backs! They also play games, such as grab-the-tail. Guenon monkeys stay up higher in the trees, but often come down to play with the swamp monkeys.

THE SAN DIEGO ZOO'S MOST FAMOUS BABY

Giant pandas live in bamboo forests in the mountains of China. The pandas are endangered, because people have used up a lot of this land. The Chinese government set up a **reserve** where the giant pandas live safely and have enough bamboo to eat. Chinese scientists and San Diego Zoo scientists are working together to save the giant pandas. The Zoo scientists asked China if they could bring two giant pandas to San Diego so that Zoo scientists could learn more about these pandas. China said yes. At the Zoo, the pandas had a baby named Hua Mei. Not many pandas are born in zoos, so this was a wonderful event. Many people came to see the baby panda, including China's **consul general**, An Wenbin.

Hua Mei is Chinese for "China USA." It also means "splendid beautiful." Hua Mei is a very important young panda!

Lizards use their tongues to help them smell. This quince monitor is sniffing to see what his keeper brought him for dinner.

Don't eat me! This poison dart frog's bright color warns animals not to eat it because it is poisonous.

In the Reptile House

The San Diego Zoo has more than 1,000 reptiles and **amphibians**. In the Reptile House in the Zoo's southeast area, you can see giant Galápagos tortoises and rattlesnakes. There are frilled lizards that can run on their hind legs, snapping turtles, and all kinds of frogs. All reptiles are cold-blooded. That means their bodies are the same temperature as the air around them. They need warmth for the energy to move around. That is why reptiles often rest in sunny spots. The animals in the Reptile House get their warmth from special lamps and also from windows in the roof that let in the sunshine. Their houses have rocks, pools, trees, and other natural things found where reptiles live in the wild.

KAREN'S HEART

Sometimes animals get sick or hurt. Then the Zoo's **veterinarians** take care of them. One special patient was Karen the orangutan. She was born at the Zoo and was raised in the nursery. She seemed healthy at first, but then the Zoo staff noticed she wasn't growing the way she should.

The veterinarians gave her a check-up and found out she had a hole in her heart, something that humans can be born with, too. She needed surgery to fix it. The veterinarians came up with a plan. They called some doctors who do special surgery on human children and asked them to help fix Karen's heart. It worked! The doctors closed the hole, and Karen got well.

The word "orangutan" means "man of the forest." The people who named orangutans thought that they looked like wise old men hiding in the trees.

Before her operation, Karen wasn't growing the way she should have been.

After her operation, Karen received cards and get-well wishes. Today Karen is a healthy adult. She lives with the other orangutans near the center of the Zoo.

DEAR KAREN,
WE hope you'Re
back out in the
sunshine

15

This gorilla enjoys a fruit popsicle on a hot summer day.

PLAYING, THINKING, AND LEARNING

Do you get bored when there's nothing to do? That happens to zoo animals, too. They are well cared for because they have food, shelter, and healthcare, but they still need to be busy and active. That's why San Diego Zoo zookeepers give them things to play with, places to explore, food to hunt for, friends to live with, and challenges to think about. This is called **enrichment**. The keepers leave a trail of smells for a hyena to sniff out in its exhibit. They give branches to deer to thrash with their horns. They hide fruit for gorillas to find and eat. When animals explore and learn new things, their lives are better. You can give your own pets enrichment. Playing catch with your dog or wiggling a string for your cat is enrichment!

When Dr. Charles Schroeder was the director of the San Diego Zoo, he imagined another wildlife park that was part of the Zoo, but in a different place. It would have open fields where herds of giraffes, rhinos, antelope, buffalo, and other animals roamed together. Visitors would see the animals from a train.

In 1972, his dream came true. The San Diego Wild Animal Park opened on 1,800 acres (728 ha) of land 30 miles (48 km) northeast of the Zoo. Herds of animals roam the Park's fields, just as Dr. Schroeder imagined. Visitors can also see warthogs, okapis, bighorn sheep, California condors, red river hogs, and shoebill storks up close. They can even feed giraffes. It's pretty wild!

Giraffes are the tallest land animals on Earth.
Their tongues are almost 2 feet (.6 m) long!

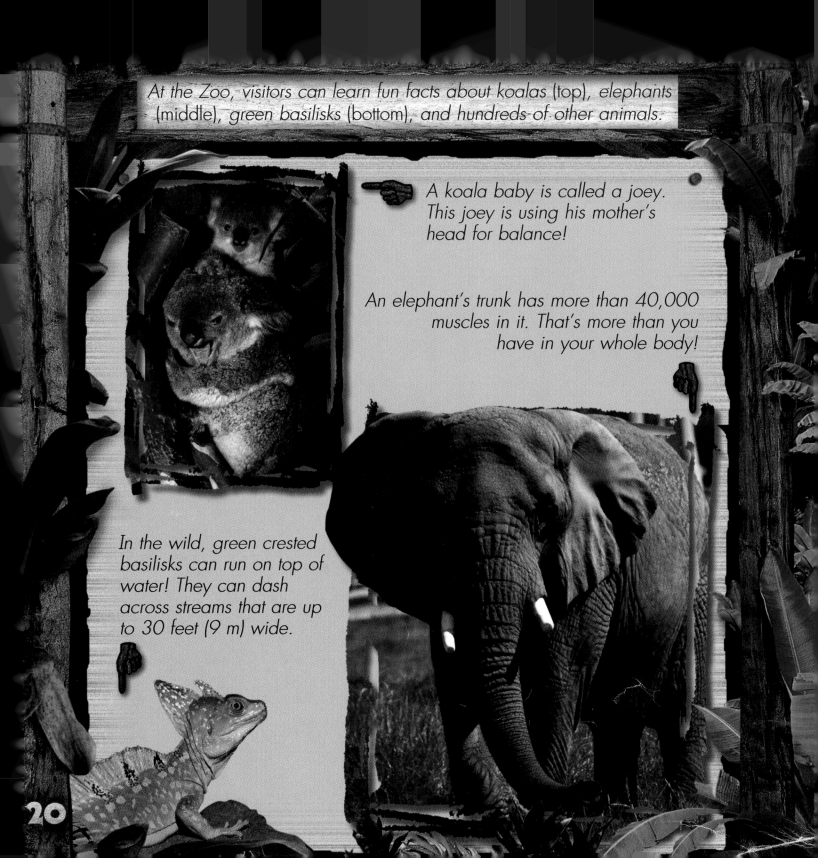

At the Zoo, visitors can learn fun facts about koalas (top), elephants (middle), green basilisks (bottom), and hundreds of other animals.

A koala baby is called a joey. This joey is using his mother's head for balance!

An elephant's trunk has more than 40,000 muscles in it. That's more than you have in your whole body!

In the wild, green crested basilisks can run on top of water! They can dash across streams that are up to 30 feet (9 m) wide.

WILD AND WEIRD ANIMAL FACTS

The world of wildlife is full of wild, weird, and wonderful facts. For instance, if you tell a koala, "Go eat dirt!" you won't hurt its feelings. Sometimes koalas eat a little dirt after they've finished eating their eucalyptus leaves. It helps them to digest their food.

It's impossible to walk on water unless you're a water bug, right? Wrong! Green crested basilisks can run across water when they're in trouble. It's a handy way to escape **predators**.

When your stomach growls, it usually means you are hungry. When an elephant uses its throat to make a similar sound, it is a signal to other elephants that everything is okay. These are just a few of the strange animal facts that you can learn at the San Diego Zoo!

SAVING ANIMALS

One of the San Diego Zoo's main jobs is to save animals. Zoo specialists travel all over the world to protect animals from **extinction**. They care for some animals at the Zoo, where the animals can live safely and can have babies. They help to set up reserves in the animals' native countries so that animals can live there safely. They also teach people to protect the animals that live around them.

One of the Zoo's rescue projects is in the Caribbean Islands. Dr. Allison Alberts works with a team that is saving the islands' rock iguanas. The large lizards were almost extinct when her team came. Now the rock iguanas are doing better. The Zoo will continue to work to save animals for the future.

amphibians (am-FIH-bee-unz) Animals that live in the water as babies and on land as adults. Frogs are amphibians.

consul general (KAHN-sul JEN-rul) A very important official sent by his or her government to a foreign country to represent the home country.

endangered (en-DAYN-jerd) In danger of no longer existing.

enrichment (in-RICH-mint) Objects and activities that keep animals active and challenged.

exhibits (ig-ZIH-bits) Displays designed for people to come and see.

extinction (ik-STINK-shun) The state of no longer existing. If a species of animal is extinct, it means the last one of its kind has died.

predators (PREH-duh-terz) Animals that kill other animals for food.

reserve (rih-ZURV) A place where animals and plants are safe in the wild. For example, Yellowstone National Park is a reserve for the plants and animals that live there. People can visit, but they are not allowed to build houses there or to take home the plants or the animals.

species (SPEE-sheez) One kind of plant or animal.

subspecies (SUB-spee-sheez) Types within a species. For example, Siberian tigers and Sumatran tigers are subspecies of tigers. The Siberian tiger's fur is longer and thicker and looks different from the Sumatran tiger's fur.

tropical rain forest (TRAH-pih-kul RAYN FOR-est) Warm, wet forests located in the warmest areas of Earth near the equator.

veterinarians (veh-tuh-ruh-NEHR-ee-enz) Doctors who treat animals.

INDEX

A

Alberts, Dr.
    Allison, 22

E

endangered, 6
enrichment, 17
extinction, 22

H

Hua Mei, 10

I

Ituri Forest exhibit, 9

K

Karen the
    orangutan, 14

P

Panama-California
    International
    Exposition, 5
predators, 21
Prince the lion, 5

R

Reptile House, 13
reserve(s), 10, 22

S

San Diego Wild
    Animal Park,
    18
Schroeder, Dr.
    Charles, 18

V

veterinarians, 14

W

Wegeforth, Dr.
    Harry M., 5
Wenbin, An, 10

WEB SITES

Due to the changing nature of Internet links, PowerKids Press has developed an online list of Web sites related to the subject of this book. This site is updated regularly. Please use this link to access the list:
www.powerkidslinks.com/gzus/sandiegz/